SCHIRMER'S LIBRARY
OF MUSICAL CLASSICS

THEODOR KULLAK

The School of Octave-Playing

A Supplement to the Method of Modern Piano-Playing

Section I: PRELIMINARY SCHOOL
Exercises for Developing the Hands for Octave-Playing
Library Vol. 475

Section II: SEVEN OCTAVE-STUDIES
Library Vol. 476

Biographical Sketch of the Author,
and Translations by
DR. THEODORE BAKER

G. SCHIRMER, Inc.

DISTRIBUTED BY

Copyright, 1898, by G. Schirmer, Inc.
Copyright renewal assigned, 1926, to G. Schirmer, Inc.
Printed in the U. S. A.

The sign (') frequently occurring in the following studies, and called by me in its present use a comma, indicates that the hand is permitted, even where no rest is marked, to sever the connection of the tones by lifting — by taking breath, as it were. This separation must, of course, be extremely brief — the least instant of time — so as not to interrupt the rhythm; but long enough to carry the hand from one key to the next, so that it stands directly over the latter before the note is struck. For the wider intervals this is especially necessary, or at least advantageous, in order not to strike false notes, but to effect the widest leaps with ease and certainty.

Part Second.

Seven Octave-studies.

The preliminary exercises for this study are found in Part I, Section I, of the School of Octave-playing, more especially under Nos. 1 and 4. The study itself should be executed with the utmost possible repose, great lightness, and with elegance and grace rather than passionate vehemence. When one and the same octave is uninterruptedly repeated for a long time, e. g., at the beginning of the second part of the study, and in the closing part, fatigue will be avoided by observing what was said in the "Preparatory Exercises" concerning the equal rise and fall of the wrist.

I.

Copyright, 1898, by G. Schirmer, Inc.   Printed in the U. S. A.   Copyright renewal assigned, 1926, to G. Schirmer, Inc.
13859 X

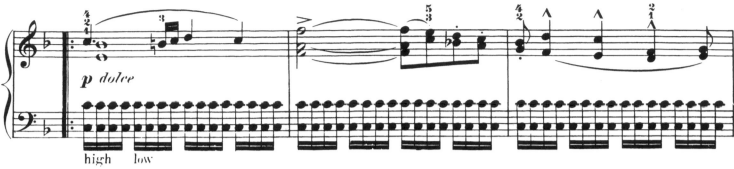

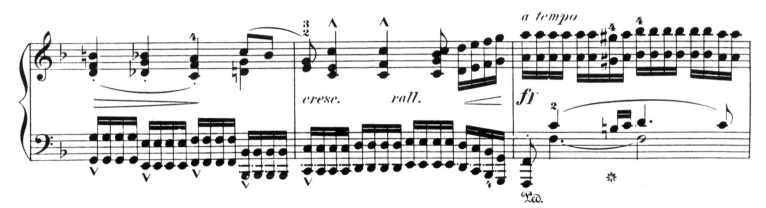

II.

Same preliminary exercises as for Study № **1.** 1, of the "School of Octave-playing."
Pay special attention to № **4** in Part I. Section,

Allegro scherzando.

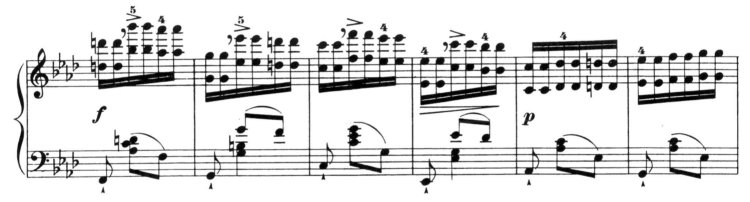

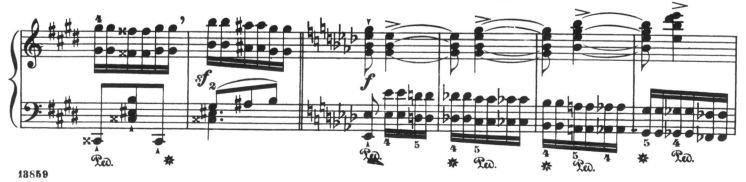

13859

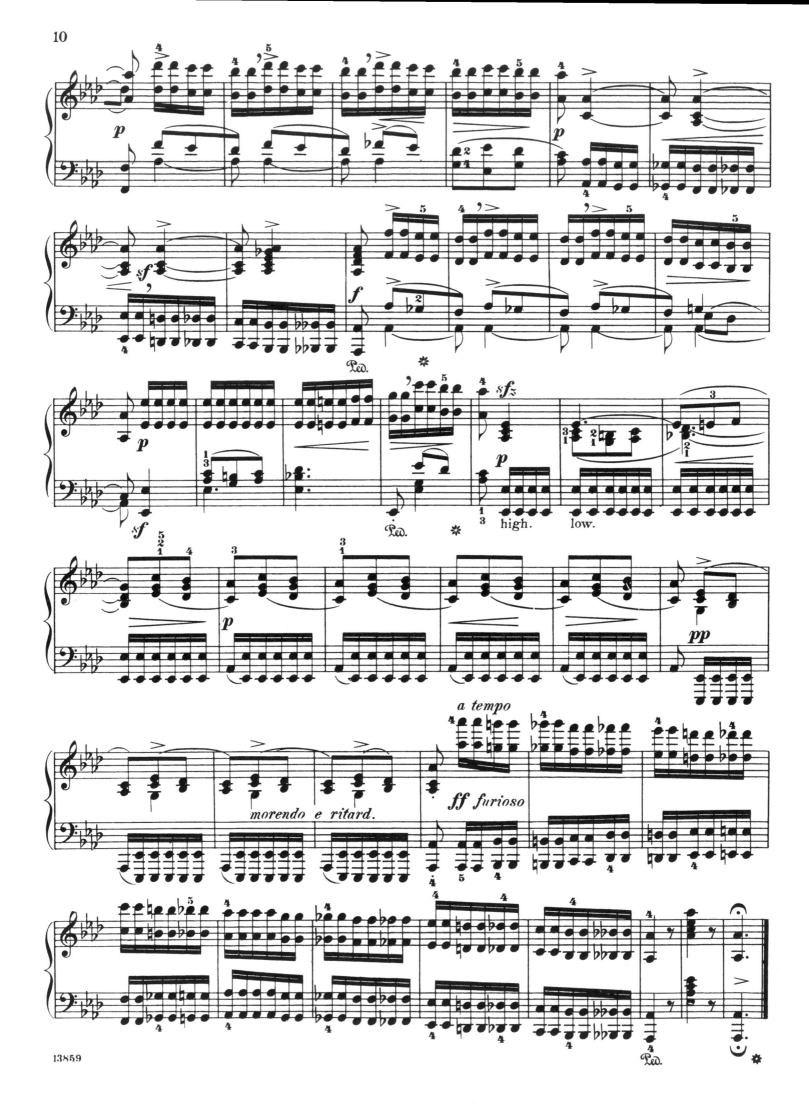

III.

Preliminary exercises, № 2, in Part I, Section 1, of the "School of Octave-playing."

Andante legato assai.

12

IV.

Preliminary exercises: Scale-playing, in Part I, Section 2, of the "School of Octave-playing."

Allegro con fuoco.

13859

Regarding the execution of legato octaves in chromatic succession, compare with № 2, in Part I, Section 1, "School of Octave-playing."

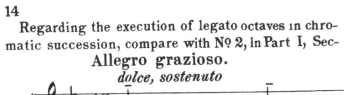

Allegro grazioso.

dolce, sostenuto

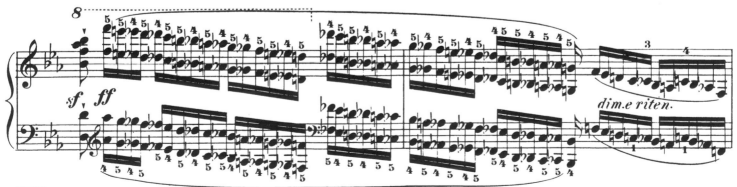

Tempo I.

dolce, sostenuto

VI.

When chords alternate with simple octaves, as in this study, play the chords by pressing the keys down (i.e., with the pressure-touch), and the simple octaves by striking (i.e., with the wrist-stroke).

Allegro maestoso.

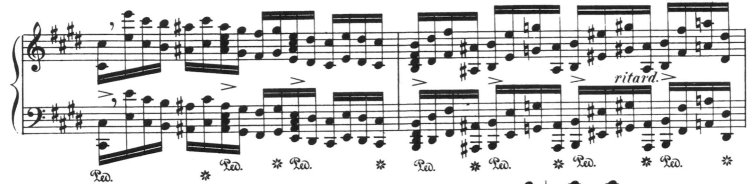

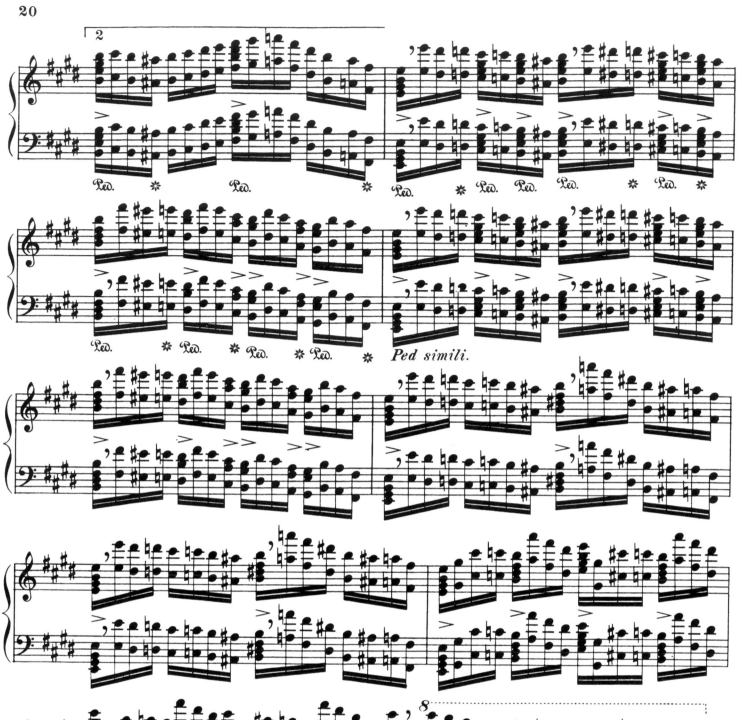

VII.

Preliminary exercises: Nᵒˢ 6 and 7, in Part I, Section 2, of the "school of Octave-playing."

Meno Allegro e maestoso.

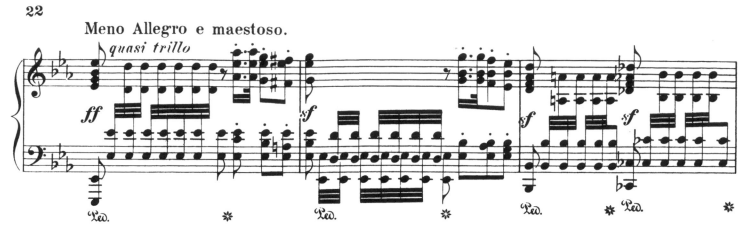

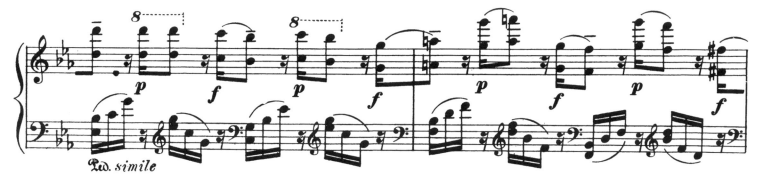

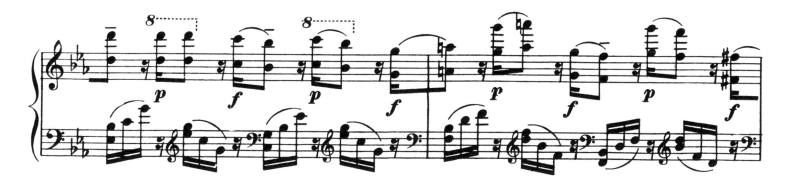

Tempo I.

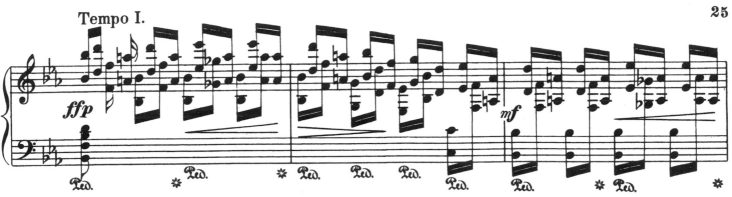

13859

Meno Allegro e maestoso.

13859

Tempo I.

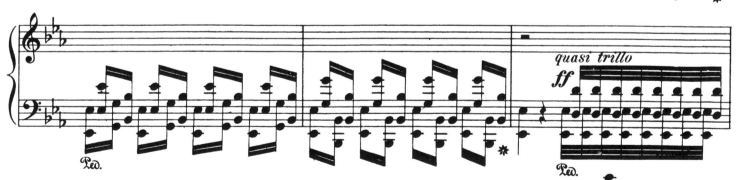